I'll Have What *She* Had

(extra grace on the side, please!)

A 21-Day Devotional Journey

with the Realest Women in Scripture

By Kimberly Billings

FAVOR DEI
PRESS
NEW YORK

I'll Have What *She* Had
(extra grace on the side, please!)

A 21-Day Devotional Journey
with the Realest Women in Scripture

First Edition

Cover Designer: Kimberly Billings

ISBN: 979-8-9993690-0-0

Printed in United States of America

Table of Contents

Dedication

Introduction

Day 1: Eve - *The First Woman to Believe a Lie*

Day 2: Sarah - *Laughing in the Face of God's Timeline*

Day 3: Hagar – *The Girl Who Was Seen*

Day 4: Rahab - *The Brave Woman with a Shady Rep*

Day 5: Ruth – *The Loyal Outsider with a Bold Yes*

Day 6: Naomi - *The Woman Who Called Herself Bitter*

Day 7: Hannah - *The Woman Who Prayed Like She Meant It*

Day 8: Abigail - *The Woman Who Kept the Peace (& Her Head)*

Day 9: Esther - *The Queen Who Chose Courage Over Comfort*

Day 10: Mary - *The Girl Who Said Yes to the Impossible*

Day 11: Elizabeth - *The Woman Who Waited Well and Blessed Loud*

Day 12: Mary of Bethany - *The One Who Chose Worship Over Worry*

Day 13: Martha - *The Woman Who Spoke Faith While Still Hurting*

Day 14: The Samaritan Woman - *The Outsider Who Became a Messenger*

Day 15: The Bleeding Woman - *The One Who Reached Out When She Had Nothing Left*

Day 16: The Canaanite Woman - *The One Who Fought with Faith and Didn't Back Down*

Day 17: Mary Magdalene - *The One Who Stayed When It Got Really Bad and Ran to Tell the Good News*

Day 18: Lydia - *The Businesswoman Who Opened Her Heart and Her Home*

Day 19: Priscilla - *The Woman Who Taught the Word and Built the Church*

Day 20: Lois & Eunice - *The Women Who Passed Down a Legacy of Faith*

Day 21: She Believed God (Wrap-Up) - *When Faith Isn't Fancy but Still Sticks*

Epilogue

Let's reflect

Blessing Prayer

From Devotional to Daily

Dedication

To all my sisters, those who I know and those I have yet to meet, to the women who have gone before us and the women still to come. No matter where you are on your faith journey, I pray that you may know that you are *seen*, *chosen*, and *deeply loved* by the God who calls you His daughter.

Introduction

Why I Wrote This & Why You're Here (I hope!)

Let me just say this up front: I didn't write this book because I have it all together. I wrote it because I clearly *do not*.

I've doubted like Sarah.

I've run like Hagar.

I've gotten myself all in a useless tizzy like Martha, prayed like Hannah, waited like Elizabeth, and wanted to disappear like the bleeding woman.

I've made bad decisions and screwed things up BAD like Eve. I've wrestled with shame, with silence, and with comparison, with feeling invisible, not-enough, and sometimes too-much.

Yeah, well, guess what? So did the women in this book.

That's why I felt called to study them and write their stories. These aren't just "Bible women" in some Sunday school kids' lesson. They were *real* women, with *real* stories, *real* challenges, and *real* faith that held them together; not because they were perfect, but because their God was faithful.

As I studied, I was able to see myself in every single one of them. Most of the time it wasn't the good in them that I saw, but the rough in their stories. I knew I had some work to do.

I identified with the weak moments, the sassy replies, the panic, the pushing, the weeping, the "Lord, are You kidding me right now with this?" prayers.

That's what this journey is: it's a slow, honest walk through Scripture—with 21 women who weren't always brave, bold or polished, but who were chosen, seen, heard, forgiven, and used by God as examples of His faithfulness to us. Woo-hoo! You go, girls!

So, what happens on Day 21? It's your turn. After all, you are one of the women who believes God (and you already bought this book, so, you might as well keep going).

Why I Pray This Book Helps

I pray that this 21-day journey will do for you what it's done (still doing?) for me — that it reminds you that God doesn't expect you to be superhuman. He expects you to be His giving to Him yourself, your desire for control, your fears, anxieties, struggles, and even your dreams. He promises He is faithful, why don't we always believe that?

I hope this book lets you exhale.

Not in a cutesy, "Jesus loves you, girl!" kind of way (but yeah, He does), but in the gritty, Gospel-focused, Christ-centered-doctrine kind of way that says:

You are forgiven.

You are not held together by your striving.

You are held together by the finished work of Jesus.

That's not motivational blah-blah-blah. That's *truth*.

That is why these women matter. Their stories are anchored in the same faith that anchors yours.

How to Go Through This Journey

Each day includes:

- A short Scripture reading

- A real-life retelling (with some sass, because: ME)

- A "Let's Be Real" moment that puts it in perspective

- A truth to believe... even if it's difficult to wrap your brain around it

- A guided journaling page with space for reflection, confession, celebration, and prayer

- A coloring page! Go get yourself some new colored pencils!

Take your time. Don't rush this. Sit with these women. Learn from them. Journal like no one's watching (because no one is, except Jesus, and He already knows).

You can go straight through in 21 days or hang out a bit longer studying the ones that hit hard (I certainly did... sometimes I found myself going back to re-read and make more sense of it all). You can write out prayers, draw in the margins, tape in sticky notes, cry, rant, rejoice, whatever helps you draw closer to God.

Listen, the same God who met them in the garden, at the well, in their grief, in the waiting room, and at the tomb? You betcha: He's going to meet you where YOU are.

So, game on.

Open your heart.

Turn the page.

Get yourself a favorite pen.

Let God show you His faithfulness in your life.

With love & good coffee... your sassy, overly caffeinated sister-in-Christ,

Kim

PS

Before you turn the page to Day 1, I want you to read the following below. Read it slowly. Read it out loud (if possible... if not, go in the car or something). In any case, read it *like you mean it*. It's the heart behind every chapter, every woman, and every word.

She Believed God

...not because she had it all together.
Not because she woke up flawless,
without smudged makeup or bedhead,
or never doubted, panicked, or said,
"Lord, are You for real?"

She believed God—
because *He* held her together.
This is for every woman who has ever
been through anything
close to what these women experienced
and still wondered if God was even listening.

This isn't a fairytale.
This isn't cartoonish, glitter-covered, floofy girl-power.
This is grace:
Sola Scriptura.
Sola Fide.
Sola Gratia.

Christ crucified, risen, and reigning...
for women who believe with shaking hands
and mascara-streaked faith.
This is a book about REAL women.
Messy ones. Women like us.

This is 21 days with women who didn't just believe in
God,
they took Him at His Word.
Even when it hurt.
Even when it cost them everything.
Even when it didn't make sense.

So, grab a cuppa something, hop into your favorite chair,
and grab that favorite pen I told you to get.
You bring the tears and questions; I'll bring the stories
and the sass. Ready to get your faith on? Let's go.

Day 1 – Eve: The First Woman to Believe a Lie

The original "It Girl" of humanity and the poster child for "You had one job!"

Read: Genesis 3

Scripture Focus

And the woman said to the serpent, "We may eat of the fruit of the trees in the garden, but God said, 'You shall not eat of the fruit of the tree that is in the midst of the garden, neither shall you touch it, lest you die.'" Genesis 3:2–3

Her Story, Your Reality

Eve had it all... literally! She lived in Paradise. No hormone fluctuations, no need to watch her weight, and I bet her hair was always on point. She even had the perfect husband, who was probably ripped and beyond handsome (God's image, right?), who never forgot date night (ok, well, because there was no one else on the planet), and who ALWAYS listened to her every word (Lol – had to add that). Eve was known, loved, and created with divine intention. Still... like for us sometimes, it just wasn't enough, and she wanted more.

Sound familiar?

We've all done it... stood in front of a "forbidden fruit" tree (or a storefront, or the Amazon app, or a toxic relationship) thinking, *"Maybe this thing that's off-limits is exactly what I need right now."* We know God's Word. We believe His promises. And yet... sometimes, we believe the lie anyway.

That lie, that God is holding out on us, that we're missing something, or that we need more to be more. FOMO at its finest.

And just like that, the fruit is in our hand, the bite is taken, and shame shows up like an Amazon Prime delivery—fast, free, and fully boxed-up in regret.

Let's Be Real

Eve wasn't dumb. She was deceived. There's a difference.

The enemy didn't walk up waving a red flag and saying, "Yo, Eve! Wanna ruin everything?"

Nope. He started with a question: "Did God really say...?"

Let's not pretend we're so much wiser than Eve. Most of us can't even walk past a clearance rack or scroll past an email promo without questioning God's gifts, let alone navigate relationships, parenting, grief, or that silent shame we carry.

However, the story doesn't end with Eve's failure, thank God. The same Lord who clothed her with animal skins (oh please, don't say "ew" if you own anything leather LOL) would one day clothe us in righteousness. That's grace. That's Jesus. That's the only reason we can still stand tall after the fall.

Believe This

You are not defined by the fruit you picked or the failure you fell into. You are, however, defined by the One who walked back into the garden, calling your name, even when you were hiding.

Key Word: Temptation

One-Line Summary of Her Story: The first woman believed a lie and broke the world, but God didn't leave her (or us) there.

I saw God's hand today in:

_____

_____

_____

(Even in my mess. Even in my mistakes. Even when I hid.)

Today's struggles:

_____

_____

_____

(What lie did I almost believe—or fully believe—today?)

Today's successes:

_____

_____

_____

(Big wins or tiny victories. Obedience counts, even if it's clumsy.)

What this woman teaches me:

_____

_____

_____

(Even when we screw up spectacularly, God shows up anyway.)

Key truth I'm holding on to:

_____

_____

_____

(Shame is loud, but grace speaks louder.)

How I can live this out today:

_____

_____

_____

(Run to God instead of hiding. Refuse to let shame write my story.)

My prayer:

_____

_____

_____

(Tell Him what tempts you. He's not shocked. He already knows.)

Temptation

Day 2 – Sarah: Laughing at God's Timeline

The original queen of the eye roll who laughed at God's plan... and still got a heaping scoop of His faithfulness.

Read: Genesis 18:10–15, 21:1–7

Scripture Focus

"Is anything too hard for the Lord?" Genesis 18:14a

Her Story, Your Reality

Homegirl was pushing 90 when God told her she'd finally get the baby she'd been praying for. What did she do? She laughed. Not a cute, little chuckle. Not a joyful cheer either. No, Sarah probably straight-up snorted in laughter from her disbelief at what could only be considered absurd.

My husband loves to say the phrase: Man plans, God laughs. When God gives us a path that doesn't line up with our reality (or our timeline) our first response isn't always worship. With me, it's likely sarcasm. Sometimes it's the kind of scoff that says, "Yeah, okay, God. Sure."

Sarah had waited decades. Those decades (DECADES!) were filled with hope and heartbreak, month after month, year after year. In that waiting, she tried to help God out (hi, Hagar). Spoiler: it backfired. Stay tuned for that story.

Anyway, here's the twist: God didn't take her laughter as rebellion or disrespect (although, I imagine there may have been a head shake and a face palm involved). God did not revoke His promise. He asked Sarah, gently but firmly:

[Silly woman] "Is anything too hard for the Lord?" Genesis 18:14

Ok, I added that first part. Sorry, God. Anyway, guess what? A year later, baby Isaac (whose name literally means laughter... no, really! Look it up!) was in her arms. Sarah must have busted out a joyful howl this time. The kind of laughter that bubbled up from relief, redemption, and realization that God wasn't late, He was right on time.

Let's Be Real

We want control. We want timelines. We want the thing on Amazon Prime "Get it today". Look, living by faith doesn't work like that. God doesn't hand out tracking numbers for His promises.

Sarah laughed... and she still received the promise. That means there's room for us to be imperfect and still be part of God's plan.

Believe This

God isn't offended by your doubts. He's just not limited by them.

Key Word: Laughter

A One-Line Summary of Her Story: She laughed at God's timing... and then laughed with Him when the promise finally came true.

I saw God's hand today in:

_____

_____

_____

(Was it in the delay? The unexpected encouragement? The thing you didn't think would ever happen?)

Today's struggles:

_____

_____

_____

(Still waiting? Still doubting? Still wondering if He remembers?)

Today's successes:

_____

_____

_____

(Small steps of faith. Big moments of trust. Even choosing not to spiral counts.)

What this woman teaches me:

_____

_____

_____

(Imperfect faith still lands in the middle of God's perfect plan.)

Key truth I'm holding on to:

_____

_____

_____

(God's promises don't expire just because my hope feels worn out.)

How I can live this out today:

_____

_____

_____

(Trusting the process, even when I don't understand the pace.)

My prayer:

_____

_____

_____

(Honest words. Ugly cries. Laugh-through-the-tears kind of prayer. He hears it all.)

Is anything too hard for the Lord?

GENESIS 18:14

Day 3 – Hagar: The Girl Who Was Seen

Every woman who's ever felt invisible, used, discarded, or desperate needs to meet the God who sees her

Read: Genesis 16

Scripture Focus

So, she called the name of the Lord who spoke to her, "You are a God of seeing," for she said, "Truly here I have seen him who looks after me." Genesis 16:13

Her Story, Your Reality

Hagar wasn't part of Sarai's original plan. She was the last-ditch effort backup. When Sarai couldn't conceive, Hagar, Sarai's servant, was used to "help" by giving her a child through her husband, Abram. Sadly, Hagar was treated horribly by Sarai and was discarded the minute she wasn't "needed" anymore.

Pregnant, alone, and on the run, Hagar stopped near a spring; she hormonal, of course, but also emotionally and physically wrecked. However, right there, in the middle of nowhere, an angel of God showed up.

Not to shame her or scold her.

Just to see her.

He called her by name (something she clearly needed... keep reading, it gets better) and gave her hope for the baby she carried. The angel told her that God knows what she's been through, but she needs to snap out of it and go back to Sarai (imagine hearing that bombshell). Our most gracious God would then reveal to her how she would be blessed in the future, and Hagar, this insignificant, broken woman, gave to God a name that no one had ever used before: El Roi—the God of Seeing.

Again, He saw her.

Let's Be Real

There are moments we feel invisible, forgotten, even used. Maybe not by a person like Sarai, but by life, by expectations of others, or by those in our lives who we think see us.

Hagar's story says you're never out of God's line of sight. When you're running, He sees and is right beside you (outpacing, maybe... sorry not sorry... it's God). He sees you when you're crying and when you're wondering whether you matter to anyone at all.

Believe This

God doesn't just notice you. He sees you—with compassion, intention, and love that calls you by name. Even though you sometimes feel invisible, unwanted, unimportant, not to mention unloved or unlovable. We've all been there but so was He. Face it, our sinful selves need to be reminded repeatedly that we matter—not because of who we are to others, but because of who we are to God.

Key Word: Seen

A One-Line Summary of Her Story: Cast aside and alone, Hagar met the God who saw her when no one else did.

I saw God's hand today in:

_____

_____

_____

(In the quiet? In the chaos? In the moment I almost gave up?)

Today's struggles:

_____

_____

_____

(Feeling overlooked? Unappreciated? Unworthy? You're not alone.)

Today's successes:

_____

_____

_____

(Did you get back up? Say no when you usually say yes?
Let yourself rest?)

What this woman teaches me:

_____

_____

_____

(Even when I feel forgotten, God is looking straight at
me—with love.)

Key truth I'm holding on to:

_____

_____

_____

(God sees me. Not the curated version. The real, messy,
weary me.)

How I can live this out today:

_____

_____

_____

(Stand a little taller. Speak a little kinder—to yourself and others.)

My prayer:

_____

_____

_____

(Honest. Hurting. Hopeful. Say what you need to say. He's listening.)

Day 4: Rahab: The Brave Woman with a Shady Rep

A woman with a past, a purpose, and a place in the family tree of Jesus. God doesn't just redeem reputations, He restores them.

Read: Joshua 2

Scripture Focus

"I know that the Lord has given you the land..." Joshua 2:9a

Her Story, Your Reality

Rahab was a prostitute. It's in Scripture. She lived on the edge of Jericho, not just with her home built into the city wall, but she was a social outcast, as one would imagine. She was not the type you'd expect to show up in God's story... but that's kind of God's thing.

When two Israelite dudes showed up, Rahab didn't just hide them, she confessed something shocking: she believed in their God. The God who parted the sea. The God who terrified her whole city. The God she somehow trusted to save her and her family.

Rahab was FAR from perfect. She lied. She hustled. She survived. However, when she chose faith over fear, it changed everything.

She hung a red cord in her window, just as the Israelite guys told her to do (kind of a silly act of obedience) ... until it became her rescue.

Let's Be Real

Some of us carry labels we didn't ask for. Others carry ones we earned the hard way. Either way, we all have a past. God knows, but you know that, and this is why this story is important.

Rahab didn't get a new reputation overnight. She DID, however, get a new identity: woman of faith. Not just saved but welcomed. Not just protected but honored. Her name landed in Hebrews 11 in the genealogy of Jesus.

Tell me God doesn't love to throw us a good plot twist.

Believe This

Your past may explain you, but it does not define you. Faith does that now.

We've messed up. We've carried shame. We've been labeled, dismissed, and overlooked. However, God sees something else: our faith. He sees our potential. He sees a daughter He died to redeem. No mistake is too big for God's mercy.

Key Word: Redeemed

A One-Line Summary of Her Story: A woman with a past believed boldly—and God made her part of His promise.

I saw God's hand today in:

_____

_____

_____

(In second chances? In being brave when it scared me? In the unexpected rescue?)

Today's struggles:

_____

_____

_____

(Shame that lingers? Fear of the future? Feeling like your past is louder than your faith?)

Today's successes:

_____

_____

_____

(Speaking truth? Trusting God when it was risky? Choosing courage instead of comfort?)

What this woman teaches me:

_____

_____

_____

(Faith is louder than my reputation. And obedience [even when it feels awkward] matters.)

Key truth I'm holding on to:

_____

_____

_____

(God writes new stories for women with messy pasts and brave hearts.)

How I can live this out today:

_____

_____

_____

(Leave the shame behind. Hang the cord. Say the hard truth. Walk into the unknown.)

My prayer:

_____

_____

_____

(Honest, bold, and unfiltered. Ask for redemption. Thank Him for rewriting the story.)

Day 5: Ruth - The Loyal Outsider with a Bold Yes

The ride-or-die woman of the Old Testament who teaches us that loyalty, loss, and love can all be part of God's bigger plan.

Read: Ruth 1:1-18

Scripture Focus:

"For where you go I will go, and where you lodge, I will lodge. Your people shall be my people, and your God my God." Ruth 1:16

Her Story, Your Reality

Ruth was a Moabite. Translation: not one of God's people. She had every reason to go back to what was comfortable after her husband died. Her future was uncertain, her security was gone, and Naomi—her mother-in-law—was bitter, broke, and heading into more unknown.

Ruth said yes anyway.

She walked away from her homeland. She followed grief into a foreign land. She chose faithfulness over convenience. And in the most unglamorous season of her life, she showed up every day to pick up leftovers in a field—until God showed up with something far better.

Spoiler alert: the girl who didn't belong ended up in the line of Jesus.

Let's Be Real

Faithfulness doesn't always look flashy. Sometimes it's just showing up again when everything feels uncertain. It's doing the hard, unsexy, sacrificial thing because your spirit whispers, "Stay. Go. Trust. Keep moving."

We all hit crossroads where we have to decide: go back to what's familiar, or move forward with faith into the unknown?

Ruth walked into redemption, but it started with obedience.

Believe This

God honors the bold yes, even when it's whispered through tears and fear. We don't know where God is leading us. Sometimes it's scary. Sometimes it hurts. Like Ruth, we want to obey and say "yes". Yes to staying. Yes to trusting. Yes to walking into fields that feel empty, believing God will provide.

Key Word: Faithfulness

A One-Line Summary of Her Story: Ruth said yes to faithfulness in loss—and walked straight into redemption.

I saw God's hand today in:

_____

_____

_____

(In the ordinary. In loyalty. In something small but
sacred.)

Today's struggles:

_____

_____

_____

(Fear of the unknown? Missing what you left behind?
Wondering if obedience is worth it?)

Today's successes:

_____

_____

_____

(Choosing loyalty. Showing up. Saying yes even when you
were scared.)

What this woman teaches me:

_____

_____

(Sometimes the bravest thing is to keep walking forward, even when you don't know what's next.)

Key truth I'm holding on to:

_____

_____

_____

(God honors the quiet yes and blesses faithfulness in hidden places.)

How I can live this out today:

_____

_____

_____

(Choose presence. Be loyal. Stay open to God's unexpected provision.)

My prayer:

_____

_____

_____

(Lord, help me be faithful. Help me follow even when it

feels hard or slow. Help me trust that the story's not over.)

"Where you go I will go, and where you lodge I will lodge."

RUTH 1:16

Day 6: Naomi The Woman Who Called Herself Bitter

Because sometimes grief doesn't just knock the wind out of you... it tries to rename you.

Read: Ruth 1:19-22

Scripture Focus

"Do not call me Naomi; call me Mara, for the Almighty has dealt very bitterly with me." Ruth 1:20

Her Story, Your Reality

Naomi lost everything. Her husband. Her two sons. Her hope. When she came home to Bethlehem after years away, she didn't stroll in with confidence—she dragged her grief behind her like a suitcase full of bricks.

She even told people to stop calling her Naomi, which means "pleasant," and start calling her Mara—bitter.

Ever been there?

When it feels like God emptied your hands and left you holding disappointment?

But here's the thing: Naomi's story didn't end in bitterness. She returned home in heartbreak, but she was never truly alone. Ruth stayed. God moved. And the woman who once believed her life was over ended up cradling her grandson—Obed—in her arms, the beginning of a legacy that would lead to King David... and eventually Jesus.

Naomi couldn't see the redemption coming. But it came anyway.

Let's Be Real

Grief is loud. Disappointment is heavy. Sometimes it's easier to wear bitterness like a name tag than to keep hoping for something better.

God doesn't rename us based on our worst season. He's not afraid of our honesty. Bottom line: He's not done, even when we feel we are.

Believe This

Bitterness doesn't have the final word. God does. And He still writes beauty into broken places.

We've carried bitterness. If you're anything like me, you've believed the lie that He left you empty. But here you are (look at you!), still showing up, still hoping He's not finished with you.

Key Word: Bitterness

A One-Line Summary of Her Story: Naomi came home bitter and broken—but God hadn't stopped working behind the scenes.

I saw God's hand today in:

_____

_____

_____

(In my grief? In my healing? In something that felt like a whisper of hope?)

Today's struggles:

_____

_____

_____

(Holding on to hurt? Feeling like God forgot you? Wanting to rename your season something darker?)

Today's successes:

_____

_____

_____

(Choosing to be honest. Coming home anyway. Not giving up—even when bitter felt easier.)

What this woman teaches me:

_____

_____

_____

(God doesn't cancel the story just because I'm in a chapter I hate.)

Key truth I'm holding on to:

_____

_____

_____

(Bitterness may visit, but it doesn't get to move in permanently.)

How I can live this out today:

_____

_____

_____

(Name the pain—but don't let it rename you.)

My prayer:

_____

_____

_____

(Pour it out. All the disappointment, the weariness, the aching. He's not going anywhere.)

NAOMI

"The Almighty has dealt
very bitterly with me."

RUTH 1:20

Day 7: Hannah The Woman Who Prayed Like She Meant It

The woman who poured her heart out, ugly cried at the altar, and believed God before the miracle showed up.

Read: 1 Samuel 1 and 2:1-11

Scripture Focus

"In her deep anguish Hannah prayed to the Lord, weeping bitterly." 1 Samuel 1:10

Her Story, Your Reality

Hannah wanted a baby more than anything. But month after month, year after year, the answer was no. To make it worse, she had to share space with her husband's other wife—who had kids and a mean streak. Yeah, that kind of situation.

So, Hannah did what a lot of us do when we hit the emotional wall: she snapped.

Instead of lashing out, she broke down. In God's house. At His feet.

She didn't pray politely. She prayed from the pit—so much so that Eli the priest thought she was drunk. (Rude.)

God wasn't confused by her tears. He was moved by them.

In time, Hannah's prayer was answered. She gave birth to Samuel, the prophet who would anoint kings and change the story of Israel. But get this: she didn't just get the answer—she gave it back. She handed Samuel to God, literally. Because she knew that the point of the blessing wasn't to keep it—it was to glorify the Giver.

Let's Be Real

We know what it's like to ache for something. To want it so badly it hurts. To cry until there are no words left, only groans.

Hannah's story says: go ahead. Ugly cry. Snot and mascara and all. God can take it. He wants it. He hears you—even when you can't say it out loud.

Believe This

God doesn't dismiss the desperate. He leans in close and answers with compassion.

God knows when we're tired of pretending everything's fine. We must hold on to the belief that He sees us in the struggle. We must trust His will and be patient in the waiting. Ask God in your petitions to be able to pray like Hannah—raw, real, and without a filter. When He answers, we will praise Him and all His glory!

Key Word: Prayer

A One-Line Summary of Her Story: In her heartbreak, Hannah poured it all out—and God answered with more than she ever imagined.

I saw God's hand today in:

_____

_____

_____

(In the moment I finally let it out? In someone who listened? In the stillness that felt safe?)

Today's struggles:

_____

_____

_____

(Tired of waiting? Tired of hurting? Wondering if the silence means He stopped listening?)

Today's successes:

_____

_____

_____

(Choosing prayer over panic. Trusting Him with the deepest ache. Letting go just a little.)

What this woman teaches me:

_____

_____

_____

(God honors the prayer that comes from the bottom of my soul—not the one that sounds polished.)

Key truth I'm holding on to:

_____

_____

_____

(God hears even what I can't say out loud.)

How I can live this out today:

_____

_____

_____

(Make space to pray like I mean it—without a script, without shame, just me and God.)

My prayer:

_____

_____

_____

(Don't censor it. Don't clean it up. Just write it raw.)

Day 8 – Abigail: The Wise Woman Who Kept the Peace (and Her Head)

The woman who brought snacks, spoke truth, and saved her whole household from disaster with one gutsy move.\

Read: 1 Samuel 25

Scripture Focus

"When Abigail saw David, she quickly got off her donkey and bowed down before David with her face to the ground." 1 Samuel 25:23

Her Story, Your Reality

Abigail was stuck with a hot-tempered jerk for a husband—no, for real. His name, Nabal, meant "fool," and he lived up to it. When he insulted David, future king and current military powerhouse, he basically signed a death warrant for everyone in the household.

But Abigail?

She didn't panic.

She didn't ignore it.

She acted—quickly, wisely, and humbly.

She packed up food, jumped on a donkey, and intercepted David mid-rage with wisdom, grace, and serious courage. Her words? They hit hard. David chilled out and bloodshed was avoided. When Nabal keeled over not long after (divine smiting, anyone?), David came back—not for vengeance, but for Abigail. (Aw!)

She didn't just avoid disaster. She walked right into a new future.

Let's Be Real

We all deal with fools. We've all had moments when reacting in nastiness felt easier than responding with wisdom.

Abigail shows us how to be bold without being brutal. She shows us how to use our words—not to win an argument, but to protect what matters. And maybe most of all? She reminds us that just because you're married to chaos doesn't mean you have to live in it!

Believe This

God honors wise, courageous women who know when to speak - and how to speak life.

We pray that God grants us the wisdom to choose the right words to glorify Him and act with righteousness. We need to be bold with our faith and use our God-given wisdom to know when to step in, when to speak up, and when to just bring the bread and trust Him with the battle.

Key Word: Wisdom

A One-Line Summary of Her Story: Abigail used courage and kindness to stop a battle—and saved her whole household.

I saw God's hand today in:

_____

_____

_____

(In a moment where peace was possible? In the words I almost said—or didn't?)

Today's struggles:

_____

_____

_____

(Dealing with difficult people? Holding back the urge to clap back? Trying to choose wisdom over sarcasm?)

Today's successes:

_____

_____

_____

(Spoke with grace? Took a breath before reacting? Packed spiritual snacks instead of throwing emotional grenades?)

What this woman teaches me:

_____

_____

(Wisdom doesn't mean weakness. And courage can be soft-spoken but world-changing.)

Key truth I'm holding on to:

_____

_____

_____

(God honors wise words and brave hearts.)

How I can live this out today:

_____

_____

_____

(Speak life, even when it's hard. Don't match the fool—rise above it.)

My prayer:

_____

_____

_____

(Ask for discernment. For courage. For a tongue that speaks life, not heat.)

ABIGAIL

Wisdom

Day 9 – Esther: The Queen Who Chose Courage Over Comfort

The bold beauty who risked everything, not to save herself, but her people. She didn't just wear a crown, she wore courage.

Read: Book of Esther

Scripture Focus

"And who knows whether you have not come to the kingdom for such a time as this?" Esther 4:14b

Her Story, Your Reality

Esther was beautiful, yes, but she was way more just a pretty face. She was also an orphan being raised by her Uncle Mordecai, she was a Jew, and she lived in a place where she didn't have a voice; until she did.

King Ahasuerus had had it with his queen, Vashti, and her blatant disrespect for him and his rules. Apparently, she threw a party with her girlfriends, and they sat around trash-taking their men. The last straw was when the King called for Vashti to ask her what the heck she was thinking, and she refused! Yeah, she was DONE, and the king made a decree that all women must honor their husbands (all the guys liked that, I'm sure).

Anyway, King Ahasuerus needed a new queen, and he definitely wanted an upgrade. So, the powers that be, gathering up all the most beautiful young women in the area found gorgeous, sweet Esther and tossed her into a beauty contest she didn't sign up for. The chosen ladies were all set up with all the makeup, clothing, etc. they needed to make themselves look their best to be paraded in front of the king. You guessed it, Esther wins hands down (the king was blown away by her beauty) and ends up queen of Persia.

However, just as the crown begins to settle on her head, a crisis develops: her Uncle Mordecai tells her that her people (the Jews) are marked for annihilation by Haman, one of the king's men. So, Esther has a choice: stay silent and safe in her fancy queen life or speak up and risk her life. Well, the book isn't named after her for being a coward, she chose the hard thing.

With a trembling heart and a strong spine, she said, "If I die, I die" and walked into the king's throne room uninvited (which was totally illegal). Esther did this solely by faith. Turns out it was cool because the king loved her so much and would give her anything she asked for; so, she told him the whole story and how her uncle thwarted a plot to kill him, and that it was all Haman's fault. Haman was hanged, the king saved the Jewish people, and Mordecai was honored.

Esther did what she needed to, Haman got his, and the Jews were saved.

Let's Be Real

We all have moments - "Why me?" moments.

Esther reminds us that we don't need to have all the answers, we just need to be faithful when our moment comes and trust that God knows best and has a plan. Courage isn't easy. It often feels terrifying. But you don't need a crown to have kingdom-level power. You just need a faithful heart and a God who shows up (He always will).

Face it, we're not always going to feel brave. But we CAN be faithful. We need the guts to show up when times get tough, to speak up when we'd really rather not, and to trust that God has purpose for whatever is about to go down. Faith doesn't require that we're perfect, just that we go for it.

Believe This

You were placed here, now, on purpose—for such a time as this.

Key Word: Courage

A One-Line Summary of Her Story: Esther risked her comfort and her crown to stand in the gap for her people, and God used her "yes" to save many.

I saw God's hand today in:

_____

_____

_____

(In the moment I spoke up? In an open door? In knowing
I'm not here by accident?)

Today's struggles:

_____

_____

(Fear of saying the hard thing? Wanting to hide when I
should step up?)

Today's successes:

_____

_____

(Chose obedience over comfort? Acted even when I felt
shaky? Showed up anyway?)

What this woman teaches me:

_____

_____

_____

(My moment matters. My courage matters. God placed me here on purpose.)

Key truth I'm holding on to:

_____

_____

_____

(God doesn't need me to feel brave—He just asks me to say yes.)

How I can live this out today:

_____

_____

_____

(Do the thing. Make the call. Speak the truth. Step into my "such a time as this.")

My prayer:

_____

_____

_____

(Be honest about the fear—but invite Him into it. He'll meet you right there.)

Day 10: Mary (Mother of Jesus): the Girl Who Said Yes to the Impossible

Theotokos (God-bearer or Mother of God), the one who displayed reverence, strength, and God's grace, she is a model of faith and obedience.

Read: Luke 1:26-55

Scripture Focus

And Mary said, "Behold, I am the servant of the Lord; let it be to me according to your word." And the angel departed from her." Luke 1:38

Her Story, Your Reality

Follow me with this imagery: 2000+ years ago, you're 14, still mastering your cooking and housekeeping skills, excited about your upcoming wedding to this really nice guy in town, and you get a weird visit from an angel (and yeah, you blinked and rubbed your eyes a dozen times to confirm what was right in front of you). Then he tells you God thinks you're just amazing (aka "favored") and He's going to make you pregnant with the Savior of the World – the Son of God – Emmanuel. Say what now?

You'd be cool with that, right? Especially being she was still a virgin then. No biggie...

Yeah, I'd be freaking out, too.

This wasn't just any child. This was THE Child, the foretold Messiah from the Old Testament book of Isaiah. While Mary may have been scared, confused, and probably a little overwhelmed (a little?), she responded with faith: "I am the Lord's servant."

Mary wasn't divine nor was she perfect. She wasn't chosen because she was better than anyone else. She was chosen by grace—just like we are. Her humility, faith, and obedience should be a model for all to emulate.

She believed God. I want a faith like hers!

She lived by grace through her faith in God, even when it meant rejection from family, friends, her whole town! Her confusion when the Angel Gabriel made the gender reveal was quickly followed by her complete devotion and obedience. Was Mary aware she would endure watching her Son be misunderstood, mocked, and ultimately crucified? She would bring into the world the One who would later die for the redemption of the whole people of God. Still, her faith held—not by her own strength, but through God's promises.

Let's Be Real

We love the idea of saying yes to God until it costs us something. Until it's uncomfortable. Until it feels impossible. Mary reminds us that God often uses the unexpected, the unqualified, and unprepared... not because we're worthy, but because He is gracious.

She didn't worship herself or think "Ooh, look how popular and cool I am to be favored by God!". We don't worship her, but we do honor her faith; a kind of faith that says, "Even though I am completely clueless as to why You need ME to do this, I trust You, Lord. Do what You gotta do. I'm here for it."

We won't always feel ready. We clearly don't understand God's ways. Like Mary we want to trust Him. We should pray that we are always able to say yes to His will... whether it's big, scary, or wildly unexpected. We are reminded that God doesn't call us because we're qualified - we're qualified because He calls us.

Believe This

God chooses ordinary people for extraordinary purposes—not because they're strong, but because they trust the One who is.

Key Word: Obedience

A One-Line Summary of Her Story: Chosen by grace, Mary said yes to God's impossible plan and carried the Savior into the sinful, broken world.

I saw God's hand today in:

_____

_____

_____

(In the unexpected yes? In something small that
reminded me I'm not alone?)

Today's struggles:

_____

_____

_____

(Feeling unqualified? Unnoticed? Unsure about what
God's asking me to step into?)

Today's successes:

_____

_____

_____

(Trusted God in something uncertain? Responded with
faith instead of fear?)

What this woman teaches me:

_____

_____

_____

(God's grace is what qualifies me—and obedience is the right response.)

Key truth I'm holding on to:

_____

_____

_____

(God uses ordinary women to carry out extraordinary grace.)

How I can live this out today:

_____

_____

_____

(Say yes—without needing all the answers. Trust the One who calls.)

My prayer:

_____

_____

_____

(Tell Him your "yes"—even if it comes with trembling hands. He hears.)

OBEDIENCE

Mary, Mother of Jesus

Day 11: Elizabeth: The Woman Who Waited Well and Blessed Loud

The woman who waited a lifetime, carried a miracle, and spoke blessing over someone else's promise without bitterness. filled with grace, maturity, and joy that refuses to compete

Read: Luke 1

Scripture Focus

"And blessed is she who believed that there would be a fulfillment of what was spoken to her from the Lord."—Luke 1:45

Her Story, Your Reality

Elizabeth was older when we meet her in the Gospel of Luke. I'm talking way past childbearing years. Still, month after month, year after year, she hoped. She prayed. She waited.

No baby. No answer. Just silence.

Had God forgotten her? Was He ignoring her prayer?

You've heard that expression, haven't you? He might not be saying "No" but rather "Not yet".

One day, He broke the silence. The angel Gabriel told her husband Zechariah that their son—John the Baptist—would prepare the way for the Savior. And Elizabeth? She got to carry that promise. Not just the physical child, but the *spiritual hope*.

What's even more beautiful? When pregnant Mary showed up at her door—young, not married yet, and scared—Elizabeth didn't flinch. She didn't compare. She didn't judge. She didn't get bitter that her own promise took decades while Mary's miracle came suddenly.

Instead, she blessed her.

She rejoiced for someone else's miracle—even while still wrapping her brain around her own.

Let's Be Real

Comparison is a thief. Bitterness is a bully. But blessing others? That's spiritual warfare and I want to be armed and ready!

Elizabeth could've gone into "Why not me first?" mode. But she didn't. She chose joy. She chose celebration. And in that moment, she spoke one of the most powerful encouragements in Scripture: "Blessed is she who believed."

When it's hard to be happy for others—look at Elizabeth. She shows us what it means to trust God's timing and champion other women's callings. Read that again.

Believe This

God's faithfulness to someone else isn't proof He's forgotten you—it's proof He's still in the business of miracles.

Key Word: Blessing

A One-Line Summary of Her Story: Elizabeth waited faithfully—and when her promise came, she made room to bless someone else's too.

I saw God's hand today in:

_____
_____
_____

(In the waiting? In a word of encouragement? In someone else's good news?)

Today's struggles:

_____
_____
_____

(Jealousy? Impatience? Feeling like my turn still hasn't come?)

Today's successes:

_____
_____
_____

(Spoke blessing instead of comparison? Waited with grace? Encouraged someone else while still hoping myself?)

What this woman teaches me:

_____

_____

_____

(There's enough of God's goodness to go around—and celebrating others doesn't mean I'm forgotten.)

Key truth I'm holding on to:

_____

_____

_____

(Believing God is blessing enough. I don't need to see it to speak it.)

How I can live this out today:

_____

_____

_____

(Lift someone up. Cheer someone on. Wait well—with joy.)

My prayer:

_____

_____

_____

(Honest. Hopeful. Ask for patience, and for the ability to bless others loud and real.)

Day 12 – Mary of Bethany: The One Who Chose Worship Over Worry

The woman who sat at Jesus' feet; a quiet, holy pause in the middle of the chaos, making worship so bold it made even religious people squirm.

Read: Luke 10:38-42

Scripture Focus

"Mary has chosen the good portion, which will not be taken away from her." Luke 10:42

Her Story, Your Reality

Mary of Bethany was the queen of unbothered... but in a good way.

While her sister Martha was running around cooking, cleaning, and stress-hustling to be the hostess with the mostest (#goals), Mary plopped herself down at Jesus' feet. When Martha complained (honestly relatable), Jesus didn't tell Mary to help, He told Martha to *chill*. Then, to add to the burn, He said Mary had chosen what matters most.

That wasn't the only time Mary made a bold move.

Fast forward to John 12. Jesus is at a dinner party, and what does Mary do? She takes expensive perfume (like a year's wages level of expensive) and pours it out on His feet. Then wipes it with her hair. It was shocking. Messy. Beautiful. The ultimate worship. And it ticked off the people who liked things tidy and respectable (hmm... Martha? She already had the cloth and cleaner to get all that perfume oil off the floor).

Mary didn't care. She gave Jesus everything she had. Her attention. Her dignity. Her treasure. She knew He was worth it.

Let's Be Real

We're all a little Martha inside. Distracted. Busy. Tired. Anxious. Wanting to please people more than we sit still with Jesus. (Ok, ok... those of you who know me are saying: "Oh, Kim, you're A LOT Martha inside")

However, Mary reminds us: you don't earn your spot at His feet, YOU JUST SHOW UP

She wasn't lazy. She was focused. She wasn't dramatic. She was devoted. When it came down to it, her worship didn't care what people thought—because it wasn't for *them.*

Admit it, we sometimes get distracted and tired. We let busy take over our focus. If you're like me, you want to be like Mary but you have to let go of the Martha inside. We need to pray for the strength and focus to tune out the noise, quiet the critics, and pour it all out (from our hearts... you don't actually have to pour perfume).

Believe This

Worship that costs you something is the kind that stays with Jesus forever.

Key Word: Worship

A One-Line Summary of Her Story: Mary stopped striving, sat still, and gave Jesus everything—even when others didn't understand.

I saw God's hand today in:

_____

_____

_____

(In the stillness? In the middle of the mess? In a moment when I finally stopped running?)

Today's struggles:

_____

_____

_____

(Too busy to breathe? Feeling judged for slowing down? Unsure how to just be with Jesus?)

Today's successes:

_____

_____

_____

(Made space for silence? Focused on Jesus instead of performance? Worshiped without apology?)

What this woman teaches me:

_____

_____

_____

(Presence > performance. And worship matters more than doing all the things.)

Key truth I'm holding on to:

_____

_____

_____

(Jesus doesn't ask me to impress Him. He invites me to sit with Him.)

How I can live this out today:

_____

_____

_____

(Take a breath. Light a candle. Pour something out for Jesus—your time, your heart, your focus.)

My prayer:

_____

_____

_____

(Say it slow. Say it sincerely. Even two honest words
count more than fifty fake ones.)

Day 13 – Martha: The Woman Who Spoke Faith While She Was Still Hurting

The woman who's doing all the things but also had bold faith and a front-row seat to a resurrection.

Read: John 11:1-44

Scripture Focus

She said to him, "Yes, Lord; I believe that you are the Christ, the Son of God, who is coming into the world." John 11:27

Her Story, Your Reality

Martha gets labeled the "busy one," and sure—when Jesus first came to her house, she was elbow-deep in dishes while her sister Mary chilled with the Lord in the living room. Martha got frustrated, and Jesus gently corrected her: "You are worried and upset about many things."

Same, Martha. Same.

But don't miss this: that wasn't the end of her story.

Later, when her brother Lazarus died and Jesus finally showed up four days after the funeral, it was Martha who ran out to meet Him. And in her grief, she still had the guts to say, "Even now, I believe."

She didn't understand. She didn't like the timing. But she still trusted Him.

That's faith that shows up in the middle of the mess—not just after the miracle.

And then? She watched her brother walk out of the tomb.

Let's Be Real

We've all had Martha moments—overloaded, anxious, short-tempered, and secretly annoyed that people aren't helping us carry it all.

Martha also teaches us how to believe in Jesus when things feel broken and wrong. She didn't have it all together. She didn't pretend to. Still she ran to Jesus, even in the pain.

That's what He wants.

It's easy to get upset when we're tired, carrying too much, frustrated, overwhelmed, and even disappointed with God's timing. We need to strive to be like Martha in this story – we need to run to Him even in our grief and hurt. We must never forget to pray for the words to speak faith, even when we're still waiting on the miracle.

Believe This

Jesus meets us in our doing, our doubting, our grieving—and He brings resurrection with Him.

Key Word: Faith

A One-Line Summary of Her Story: Martha was tired, grieving, and still believed - right there in the middle of the heartbreak.

I saw God's hand today in:

_____

_____

_____

(In the doing? In the moment I cried out? In the whisper of hope that showed up anyway?)

Today's struggles:

_____

_____

_____

(Too much to carry? Frustrated with others—or God? Feeling unseen in your service?)

Today's successes:

_____

_____

_____

(Spoke truth even while hurting? Let your faith speak louder than your frustration?)

What this woman teaches me:

_____

_____

_____

(Faith doesn't mean I have all the answers. It means I know who to run to.)

Key truth I'm holding on to:

_____

_____

_____

(Jesus hears me—even when I come with grief, frustration, or both.)

How I can live this out today:

_____

_____

_____

(Pause to pray before I pour out more. Trust God with the things I can't fix.)

My prayer:

_____

_____

_____

(Tell Him the truth. About the grief. The hustle. The hurt. He can handle it.)

Day 14 – The Samaritan Woman: The Outsider Who Became a Messenger

The woman with a past who met Jesus at a well and left her water jar behind because she finally found Living Water. A story for every woman who's ever believed her story disqualified her.

Read: John 4:1-42

Scripture Focus

"So the woman left her water jar and went away into town and said to the people, 'Come, see a man who told me all that I ever did. Can this be the Christ?'" John 4:28–29

Her Story, Your Reality

She came to the well alone at the middle of the day, heat blazing, shame heavy. Most women drew water in the cool of the morning, but she couldn't face the stares and whispers.

She'd had five husbands. The man she was with now wasn't her husband. She was talked about, judged, written off.

However, Jesus didn't avoid her. He waited for her.

He met her in the ordinary—just a thirsty Jewish man at a well and He offered her something deeper: Living Water. Himself.

He didn't gloss over her sin. He called her out on it - gently, directly, lovingly. He didn't use it to shame her. He used it to show her He knew her... and still loved her.

That woman – the one everyone else tried to dismiss? She ran back to town as the first evangelist in the New Testament.

Let's Be Real

We've all carried shame. We've all made choices we regret. We've all believed we're too much or not enough.

Jesus doesn't flinch at your truth. He meets you in it. He offers something better—Himself.

This woman didn't get a lecture. She got Living Water. And then? She became a voice of hope to the very people who once rejected her.

Believe This

God doesn't need your past erased to use you. He just needs your heart open to grace.

Key Word: Grace

A One-Line Summary of Her Story: A woman with a messy past met Jesus, dropped her shame, and ran to tell the truth that changed everything.

I saw God's hand today in:

_____

_____

_____

(In the middle of my routine? In a moment that felt ordinary but wasn't?)

Today's struggles:

_____

_____

_____

(Shame? Regret? Feeling like my story disqualifies me?)

Today's successes:

_____

_____

_____

(Chose grace instead of hiding? Spoke truth over my past? Took a step toward freedom?)

What this woman teaches me:

_____

_____

_____

(Jesus doesn't flinch at my truth—and I don't have to live
in shame.)

Key truth I'm holding on to:

_____

_____

_____

My past doesn't cancel my purpose. Jesus still writes the
story.

How I can live this out today:

_____

_____

_____

(Drop the jar. Stop hiding. Share something real with
someone who needs hope.)

My prayer:

_____

_____

_____

(Let it be raw. Let it be honest. Let it be full of Living Water.)

Day 16 – The Canaanite Woman: The One Who Fought with Faith and Didn't Back Down

The bold mama bear who prayed desperate prayers and refused to give up hope

Read: Matthew 15:21-28

Scripture Focus

"Even the dogs eat the crumbs that fall from their masters' table." Matthew 15:27

Her Story, Your Reality

She wasn't Jewish. She wasn't part of the "in crowd." She was a Gentile woman—already disqualified by every social and religious standard.

Her daughter was suffering, and she'd heard about Jesus.

So, she came. Loud. Desperate. Persistent.

At first, Jesus didn't answer her. Then He gave her a hard truth: *His mission was first to the lost sheep of Israel.*

Most people would've walked away right there.

Not this woman.

She replied with one of the boldest lines in Scripture: *"Even the dogs get the crumbs."*

Translation: "I know I don't deserve it. I also know who You are, and I *know* You have more than enough."

And Jesus? He didn't rebuke her. He praised her. *"Woman, you have great faith."*

Her daughter was healed that very hour.

Let's Be Real

Faith doesn't always look polite. Sometimes it's loud. Sometimes it's messy. Sometimes it's the kind that doesn't stop asking—even when the answer seems delayed.

This woman didn't get her miracle because she had the right pedigree. She got it because she knew who Jesus was—and she wouldn't let go.

That's the kind of faith that moves mountains. Or, in this case, demons.

Sometimes we may feel like outsiders. Unworthy. Ignored. However, we must *still show up*! God is SO GOOD and we know He can do whatever we're asking. We pray now that He gives us the stubborn, humble, unshakable faith it takes to go to Him!

Believe This

God honors relentless faith, not because we're entitled, but because we believe He's *that good*.

Key Word: Persistence

A One-Line Summary of Her Story: She didn't have the right background—but her faith refused to back down, and Jesus called it "great."

I saw God's hand today in:

_____

_____

_____

(In the bold prayer I whispered—or shouted? In the moment I refused to give up?)

Today's struggles:

_____

_____

_____

(Feeling overlooked? Wondering if God's silence means "no"? Fighting for someone else who's hurting?)

Today's successes:

_____

_____

_____

(Kept praying. Stayed at His feet. Claimed even a crumb of His grace.)

What this woman teaches me:

_____

_____

_____

(I don't have to be perfect to be persistent—and Jesus honors both humility and holy audacity.)

Key truth I'm holding on to:

_____

_____

_____

(God sees faith that won't let go—and He answers it with power and love.)

How I can live this out today:

_____

_____

_____

(Keep praying. Keep trusting. Keep knocking—even when the answer feels slow.)

My prayer:

_____

_____

_____

(Be bold. Be honest. Ask again. He's listening—even when it seems like He's quiet.)

HUMILITY

MATTHEW 15:21-28

Day 15 – The Bleeding Woman: The One Who Reached Out When She Had Nothing Left

The woman who reached out with trembling faith and was met with healing and dignity from the Savior who saw her.

Read: Matthew 9:20-22

Scripture Focus

"She said to herself, 'If I only touch his garment, I will be made well.'" Matthew 9:21

Her Story, Your Reality

Twelve years. That's how long she had suffered from bleeding. I can't wrap my brain around that.

She'd spent everything she had on doctors. No one could help her, nor would anyone go near her. In her culture, she was considered unclean, untouchable, unwelcome. She was an outcast.

But like the Canaanite woman, she didn't quit.

She had heard about Jesus and pushed through the crowd—risking everything—just to brush the edge of His cloak. (I'm sure she ticked off some of those judgy people, too)

When she got near enough, she reached out and touched it. Jesus stopped. She didn't just get healing, she got seen! Jesus turned around and called her "daughter." Not "unclean." Not "that woman." He gave her back her identity.

Her faith was messy, quiet, and desperate, but it was real. And Jesus honored it.

Let's Be Real

There are days when you feel like you've tried everything and nothing's changed. Days when your faith feels more like a whisper (if even that) than a war cry. I get it; you have questions.

"Doesn't God hear me?"

"What did I do to make Him not hear my prayers?"

Well, I have a sneaking suspicion that He has a question for YOU: where is *your* faith?

This woman shows us that even the tiniest reach toward Jesus isn't ignored. He doesn't just heal what's broken— He restores what shame stole.

We are not too far gone for God. We are not too messy God. We are not too tired for God. Touch the cloak of Jesus! That's enough.

Believe This

Faith doesn't have to be loud to be life-changing. Jesus sees the quiet reach—and He responds with healing.

Key Word: Healing

A One-Line Summary of Her Story: After twelve years of pain and isolation, she reached for Jesus—and He reached back with healing and dignity.

I saw God's hand today in:

_____

_____

_____

(In a tiny breakthrough? A small mercy? A reminder that I'm still seen?)

Today's struggles:

_____

_____

_____

(Tired of the wait? Feeling worn out by pain—physical, emotional, or both?)

Today's successes:

_____

_____

_____

(Reached for Jesus instead of shutting down? Let myself hope again?)

What this woman teaches me:

_____

_____

_____

(Even the smallest act of faith gets Jesus' full attention.)

Key truth I'm holding on to:

_____

_____

_____

(Jesus doesn't just heal. He restores. And He never shames the one who reaches out.)

How I can live this out today:

_____

_____

_____

(Take one step toward Him. Trust that He sees it. Let Him call me daughter.)

My prayer:

_____

_____

_____

(Pour it out. Whether it's hope or heartbreak, He's already turning toward you.)

Day 17 – Mary Magdalene: The One Who Stayed When It Got Really Bad and Ran to Tell the Good News

The woman delivered from darkness who never left Jesus' side, even when everyone else ran. She was the first witness to the resurrection. Coincidence? Not a chance. You know how I feel about coincidences.

Read: John 20:1-18

Scripture Focus

"I have seen the Lord!" John 20:18

Her Story, Your Reality

Mary Magdalene didn't just have a rough past—she had seven demons. Seven. She knew what being in bondage to sin felt like. She knew what freedom cost.

So, when Jesus healed her, Mary stuck by Him. She followed His through His ministry, through His crucifixion, through the horror of watching Him die.

While others took off, Mary stayed.

She was one of the women at the cross. One of the first at the tomb. When everyone else thought the story was over, she showed up with spices and sadness—only to be met with resurrection.

Then Jesus called her by name, and she recognized Him. Without hesitation she ran to tell the others: "I have seen the Lord."

Mary wasn't just a witness. She was pretty much the first gospel preacher! She announced his resurrection to the disciples!

Let's Be Real

Loyalty isn't loud. It shows up early, stays late, and doesn't bail when it gets bloody.

Mary Magdalene's story isn't just one of healing—it's one of devotion, commitment, love, faith, and being *called*. She knew what Jesus had saved her from, and nothing could keep her from Him—not death, not fear, not grief.

We need more of that. Not just on-the-surface faith, but stick-around, show-up, say-His-name kind of faith.

Believe This

Jesus doesn't just call the healed—He calls the faithful. He meets them with resurrection power.

Key Word: Devotion

A One-Line Summary of Her Story: Freed from darkness, Mary Magdalene never stopped following Jesus—and was the first to see Him risen.

I saw God's hand today in:

_____

_____

_____

(In something I thought was gone? In staying close when it would've been easier to walk away?)

Today's struggles:

_____

_____

_____

(Wrestling with past shame? Feeling unseen in your loyalty? Wondering if the story is really going to turn around?)

Today's successes:

_____

_____

_____

(Stayed when it got hard. Showed up when no one else did. Said His name anyway.)

What this woman teaches me:

_____

_____

_____

(My past doesn't disqualify me—devotion does more than I think it does.)

Key truth I'm holding on to:

_____

_____

_____

Jesus meets the faithful ones right in their grief—with resurrection.

How I can live this out today:

_____

_____

_____

(Stay. Watch. Speak His name. Be the one who doesn't quit when others do.)

My prayer:

_____

_____

_____

(Let it be fierce. Let it be grateful. Let it be a full-bodied "thank You for finding me.")

Day 18 – Lydia: The Woman Who Opened Her Heart and Her Home

The savvy businesswoman with a heart wide open to God and a house wide open to the Church.

Read: Acts 16:11-15

Scripture Focus

"The Lord opened her heart to pay attention to what was said by Paul." Acts 16:14b

Her Story, Your Reality

Lydia was a seller of purple cloth and that meant she had money, influence, and a killer eye for luxury textiles. She was a woman of means in a man's world, but she didn't let her wealth get in the way of her faith.

Lydia met Paul down by the river where women gathered to pray. She was already seeking truth, already spiritually curious. When Paul spoke the Gospel, God opened her heart—and Lydia said "Come on in!".

She didn't just believe, she got baptized! Then she opened up her home. Right then and there, she became the host of the first house church in Philippi.

Lydia didn't wait for permission. She used what she had—resources, leadership, hospitality— all for God's glory.

Then how cool was it that the Church grew inside her living room!

Let's Be Real

We tend to divide our lives: business over here, faith over there. But Lydia shows us that your career, your calendar, and even your couch can be holy ground!

You don't need a pulpit to make disciples. You need a heart that's open and a life that says, "Come in! Let's talk about Jesus. It's gonna be awesome, trust me."

We need to pray that God opens our hearts that way He did Lydia's. We need to see that our work, our home, maybe even our influence, can be tools to respond to His Word. Then we can welcome others in, whether it's into our space, our time, or our testimony.

Believe This

When God opens your heart, He'll open doors throughout your life. He will use you to build His Church, right where you are.

Key Word: Hospitality

A One-Line Summary of Her Story: Lydia believed the Gospel with her whole heart—and opened her home so others could believe too.

I saw God's hand today in:

_____

_____

_____

(In a conversation? In my work? In how I opened up
space for someone else?)

Today's struggles:

_____

_____

_____

(Feeling too busy to be available? Unsure how to use what
I have for God?)

Today's successes:

_____

_____

_____

(Listened well. Gave generously. Opened a door—literal
or emotional.)

What this woman teaches me:

_____

_____

_____

(Faith isn't separate from real life—it moves through it.)

Key truth I'm holding on to:

_____

_____

_____

(My space, my gifts, and my presence can be part of God's plan.)

How I can live this out today:

_____

_____

_____

(Look for one way to invite someone in—to my home, my time, my table, or my story.)

My prayer:

_____

_____

_____

(Ask God to open your heart, your hands, and your door. He'll fill what you offer.)

Day 19 – Priscilla: The Woman Who Taught the Word and Built the Church

The bold, brilliant woman who teamed up with her husband to teach the Gospel and build the early Church.

Read: Acts 18:24-28

Scripture Focus

"... they took him aside and explained to him the way of God more accurately." Acts 18:26

Her Story, Your Reality

Priscilla wasn't on stage with a mic. She wasn't loud. However, make no mistake: she knew the Word, lived the Word, and taught the Word.

Priscilla and her husband, Aquila, were tentmakers by trade and Gospel workers by heart. When a passionate preacher named Apollos came on the scene (full of zeal but lacking in critical truth) Priscilla and Aquila didn't embarrass him. They invited him in and explained the full truth of Christ *with clarity and grace.*

Priscilla didn't go viral. She didn't claim the spotlight. Her faith shaped preachers, planted churches, and strengthened believers. She used her mind, her marriage, and her home for kingdom impact.

Let's Be Real

Not every woman is called to lead from the front lines. However, every woman is called to *know* the truth, *live* it boldly, and *share* it when the moment comes.

Priscilla didn't preach from a pulpit; she discipled from her dinner table. She worked behind the scenes and left a legacy that changed lives.

You don't need permission to open your Bible, open your home, and pour into the people God puts in your path.

You can still be a quiet teacher, a faithful woman, bold and gentle. Be faithful in all times and places so He can use your words, your home, and your hands to build His church.

Believe This

You don't have to be loud to be powerful. Quiet obedience with clear truth is kingdom work.

Key Word: Truth

A One-Line Summary of Her Story: Priscilla used her knowledge, her voice, and her home to teach truth and strengthen the Church.

I saw God's hand today in:

_____

_____

_____

(In a conversation? A chance to speak truth? A quiet moment of obedience?)

Today's struggles:

_____

_____

(Feeling overlooked? Afraid to speak up? Unsure if I know enough to help someone else?)

Today's successes:

_____

_____

(Taught someone something true? Encouraged a believer? Used what I know to build up instead of tear down?)

What this woman teaches me:

_____

_____

_____

(You don't need a spotlight to be a light—truth spreads through small faithfulness.)

Key truth I'm holding on to:

_____
_____
_____

(God uses everyday conversations to shape eternity.)

How I can live this out today:

_____
_____
_____

(Look for one person to encourage with truth. Use my words for kingdom good.)

My prayer:

_____
_____
_____

(Ask for clarity. For courage. For opportunities to use truth to love others well.)

Day 20 – Lois & Eunice: The Women Who Passed Down a Legacy of Faith

Generational faith and spiritual grit... whether you're a mother, mentor, spiritual sister, or all three

Read: 2 Timothy 1:3-7

Scripture Focus

"I am reminded of your sincere faith, a faith that dwelt first in your grandmother Lois and your mother Eunice and now, I am sure, dwells in you as well." 2 Timothy 1:5

Her Story, Your Reality

We don't get whole lot of information about Lois and Eunice. No big stories. No dramatic miracles. What *do* we get? One single, powerful verse that reminds us how deep and wide faithful influence can go.

Lois and Eunice believed in Jesus—and they lived it in front of Timothy. He was the future young pastor and church leader that Paul would call *"my son in the faith."* These two women didn't raise a platform. They raised a man of God.

No spotlight. No pulpit. Just sincere, lived-out faith in their home.

The kind of faith that lingers in the air after a prayer is whispered over a child.

The kind of faith that quietly shapes the next generation.

Let's Be Real

Faithfulness doesn't always look epic. Sometimes it looks like reading Scripture or a devotion with your kids. It can be praying over a teenager who's rolling their eyes. It can be refusing to give up when your family's walking away from the truth you taught them.

Lois and Eunice weren't loud—but their legacy was long-lasting.

You don't know what kind of Timothy in your own life might be watching. You don't have to be perfect to pass on a faith that's real.

Let's pray for strength to plant truth deep—even when we may not see the fruit yet. We need our faith to be real and let it leave fingerprints on the hearts of those around us. We should pray to be the kind of woman who raises up faith in others, one seed at a time.

Believe This

Faith isn't just taught—it's caught. And your quiet, steady walk might be someone else's anchor later.

Key Word: Legacy

A One-Line Summary of Her Story: Their sincere faith didn't just stay with them—it showed up in Timothy and helped build the early Church.

I saw God's hand today in:

_____

_____

_____

(In a moment of teaching? In a spiritual conversation? In a little act of faithfulness?)

Today's struggles:

_____

_____

_____

(Wondering if my efforts matter? Tired of pouring out? Worried about the next generation?)

Today's successes:

_____

_____

_____

(Taught truth today. Lived out love. Modeled faith—even when it felt small.)

What this woman teaches me:

_____

_____

_____

(Legacy isn't about fame—it's about faith passed on in real-life ways.)

Key truth I'm holding on to:

_____

_____

_____

(Faith lived out quietly still echoes loudly into the future.)

How I can live this out today:

_____

_____

_____

(Say the prayer. Teach the truth. Keep walking faithfully. Someone is watching.)

My prayer:

_____

_____

_____

(Ask God to deepen your roots—and give you courage to sow into someone else's faith.)

Day 21 – She Believed God: When Faith Isn't Fancy but Still Holds Fast

A wrap-up for the woman who's laughed, cried, confessed, wrestled, praised, waited, questioned, and believed anyway.

This is your time to reflect, rejoice, and rest in grace. This is the exhale at the end of the journey, firmly grounded in truth, soaked in faith. Or is the journey just starting?

Scripture Focus

"Blessed is she who believed that there would be a fulfillment of what was spoken to her from the Lord!" Luke 1:45

Her Story, Your Reality

We've walked with Eve in the wreckage.

We've waited with Sarah.

We cried with Hannah.

We pushed through with the Bleeding Woman.

We stood at the empty tomb with Mary Magdalene.

We've watched women doubt, worship, hide, lead, teach, risk, pour out, and stay.

And every one of them had something in common:

They believed God.

Sometimes boldly. Sometimes quietly.

Sometimes after laughing in His face or bargaining through tears.

Faith doesn't have to be perfect. It simply has to be placed on the One who is.

See, believing *in* God isn't the same as believing God.

Lots of people believe He exists. Do they BELIEVE Him and His promises? Do they even KNOW what He promises?

But the woman who believes Him and takes Him at His Word? The woman who says "yes" even when her voice shakes?

That's the woman who's blessed.

Not because she always got it right or because she earned a trophy in the Heaven Olympics. It's simply because the God she believed in is *faithful, merciful, and unchanging* (even when she is none of those things).

Here's a truth-bomb for you: Your faith doesn't save you, Jesus does. God's grace and mercy *through* your faith saves you.

> *"Even your ability to believe is a gift from the Holy Spirit"* Ephesians 2:8–9

You're not holding on to God—He's holding on to you.

That's grace. That's Gospel. That's what we are called to share.

So, when your faith *feels* small/insignificant/unseen, it's okay. It's who your faith is in that matters. He sees you; your faith is enough!

The One who died for you, rose for you, and clothes you in His righteousness? Yeah, you can believe Him. Then watch what He does in your life and how He uses you to build His kingdom.

Let's Be Real

This world's a mess. You're tired.

There's pressure to be the perfect wife, mom, employee, friend, and Sunday morning smile machine.

Remember, your identity is not in your performance. It's in Christ.

You are forgiven, called, chosen, held... all by the God who has never once broken a promise.

So, when you say: "I believe..." you're not making a statement about how strong you are. You're confessing that *His strength* is enough.

Believe This

Faith that rests in Christ—not in itself—is faith that saves. That faith is a gift. You don't have to hustle for it. You just receive it and live like it's true. Because it is.

Key Word: Faith

A One-Line Summary of Her Story: She believed—
not perfectly, but persistently, and the God she trusted
came through on every promise.

I saw God's hand today in:

_____

_____

_____

(In the big, the small, the unexpected reminder that He's
still writing my story.)

Today's struggles:

_____

_____

_____

(Still learning to let go? Still trying to believe God instead
of just believing in Him?)

Today's successes:

_____

_____

_____

(Choosing truth over lies? Resting instead of performing? Trusting the Gospel more than your grit?)

What this whole journey taught me:

_____

_____

_____

(Faith isn't about having it all together—it's about holding on to the One who holds me.)

Key truth I'm holding on to:

_____

_____

_____

(Jesus is faithful—even when my faith feels flimsy.)

How I can live this out today:

_____

_____

_____

(Walk forward, not to prove anything—but because I'm already free in Christ.)

My prayer:

_____

_____

_____

(Thank Him. Be honest. Ask for more faith. And celebrate what He's done.)

Don't worry, I didn't forget your coloring page... I made it a really good one. Turn the page!

I'll have
what she
had

extra grace on side, please

Epilogue

Now what, sister?

Well, well, well. Look who just made it through twenty-one days with some of the boldest, baddest, most beautifully flawed women in Scripture.

YOU did. Yeah, ya did!

Whether you sprinted through this like a spiritual overachiever or dragged your heart through each page like it weighed a thousand pounds. Guess what? You're here. You showed up, and that matters more than you think.

> *"For you have need of endurance, so that when you have done the will of God you may receive what is promised."* Hebrews 10:36

Let's get one thing straight before we tie a bow on this whole experience: This wasn't meant to tidy up your life. I hope you figured that out by Day 3. This wasn't a "how to get your act together and look holy doing it" kind of devotional. Nope. This was a get-in-the-trenches, wrestle-with-your-faith (Genesis 32:24-28), cry-in-the-shower, laugh-at-God's-timing, cling-to-His-promises (2 Peter 1:4) kind of journey. You didn't sign up to be perfect. You signed up to believe.

Oh, and believing? That's *not* passive. That's warfare.

> *"For we do not wrestle against flesh and blood, but against the rulers, against the authorities, against the cosmic powers over this present darkness,*

against the spiritual forces of evil in the heavenly places." Ephesians 6:12

Believing God means trusting Him when nothing makes sense, when you're exhausted, when your plans fall apart., when the doctor calls. It's trusting Him when your family disappoints you again, when you've prayed the same prayer for years and all you've gotten is silence. Believing God doesn't mean you feel strong all the time. It means you plant your feet (even when your legs are wobbly) on the truth of who He is, and you dare to say, "I'm still here. And I still believe You". Here's Habakkuk 3:17-18:

> *Though the fig tree should not blossom,*
> *nor fruit be on the vines,*
> *the produce of the olive fail*
> *and the fields yield no food,*
> *the flock be cut off from the fold*
> *and there be no herd in the stalls,*
> *yet I will rejoice in the Lord;*
> *I will take joy in the God of my salvation.*

Even if your eyeliner's running and your faith is fraying. Believe. Have faith like theirs!

Look back at these women. They didn't come with five-point plans and Instagram-worthy picture-perfect faith. They came with bleeding bodies (Mark 5:25–34), broken pasts (Joshua 2), barren wombs (1 Samuel 1:5–10), bruised reputations (Luke 7:36–50), backtalk (Genesis 18:12–15), boldness (Esther 4:16), and brave little steps that changed history.

They believed Him. And that belief turned the tides of their lives (Hebrews 11:11).

So, what now? What do *you* do with all this?

You live it out.

In your kitchen.

In your workplace.

In the Target parking lot where your toddler is screaming and your sanity is hanging on by a peppermint wrapper.

You live it when the money's tight (Philippians 4:19)

... the friendship is complicated (Proverbs 27:6)

... the diagnosis is scary (Psalm 23:4)

... when you're celebrating something no one else clapped for (Colossians 3:23–24)

... when you're showing up to church even though your heart feels numb (Psalm 42:5)

... when you're still waiting on God to move (Romans 8:25).

You don't have to be loud about it. You don't have to perform. Here's the only thing that you *do* have to do: keep believing, even when it's inconvenient or when it's quiet. Especially then (Isaiah 30:15).

Faith that only works on the mountaintop isn't faith. Real faith walks straight into the valley and says, "Even here, God is still good" (Psalm 23:4; Romans 8:28).

So yeah—go back and reread these stories if you need to. Revisit the ones that messed you up. Sit with the women who made you cry. Tape their names to your mirror if you must. You're not meant to move on and forget them— you're meant to walk like them: not perfect, not fearless, but full of faith anyway (2 Corinthians 5:7).

You are part of *their* legacy now.

- When you rise early and pray even though your eyelids are losing the battle—that's faith like Hannah (1 Samuel 1:10–11).
- When you open your home (and your fridge) for someone who needs comfort—that's faith like Lydia (Acts 16:14–15).
- When you speak up for what's right even when your voice shakes—that's Esther's crown on your head (Esther 4:14).
- When you love someone hard and fierce, even when they don't deserve it—that's Abigail's grace in your bones (1 Samuel 25:32–33).
- When you drag your weary heart to Jesus again and again—that's Mary of Bethany's devotion spilling over (Luke 10:39).
- And when you touch the hem of His garment with nothing left but desperate hope? That's the bleeding woman's miracle waiting to happen (Mark 5:28– 29).

You may not feel like one of them. But if you belong to Christ, you *are* one of them. *Their* God is *your* God. If He was faithful to them, you better believe He's going to be faithful to you (Deuteronomy 7:9)!

Now for the good part...

You get to live like it's true!

You get to walk like a woman who believes God, not just in theory, but in every ordinary, messy, beautiful day of your earthly life (James 1:22).

You keep showing up with your worship (Psalm 34:1), your weakness (2 Corinthians 12:9), your sass, your surrender.

You let grace be louder than guilt (Romans 8:1).

You let God be bigger than your doubts (Mark 9:24).

You give Him your whole, raw, real self, not because you've got it all together, but because you finally know *you don't have to* (Psalm 51:17).

He never asked you to be perfect. He asked you to trust Him (Proverbs 3:5–6).

So, take a deep breath, my sister. You've walked with some serious women of the Word; now it's your turn.

Go live out your faith like it's contagious (Matthew 5:14–16).

Go parent like you're raising warriors (Proverbs 22:6).

Go work like you've been called to that space on purpose (Ephesians 2:10).

Go rest like God is still working behind the scenes (Psalm 127:2).

Speak up (2 Timothy 1:7)

Kneel down (1 Thessalonians 5:17)

Pour out (Philippians 2:17)

Praise louder (Psalm 103:1).

Go on. Live like a woman who believes her God—even if her hands are shaking and her coffee's gone cold.

If there's one thing we've learned together, it's this:

Flawed faith is still faith. And that's exactly the kind God loves to use (1 Corinthians 1:27–29).

Let the world see it in you.

She believed God.

Faith like theirs? I'll have what *she* had (extra grace on the side, please)

Peace,

Kim

Let's reflect...

1. Which woman's story stuck with you the most—and why? What part of her faith felt familiar? What challenged you?

_____

_____

_____

_____

_____

_____

_____

2. Where do you see yourself in your current season of faith? Be honest. Are you thriving, surviving, hiding, wrestling, or somewhere in between?

_____

_____

_____

_____

_____

_____

_____

_____

3. What does "She believed God" look like in your life today? Not "believed *in* God." Believed Him. His promises. His goodness. His timing.

_____

_____

_____

_____

_____

_____

4. What are you still praying for, even if your faith is frayed? Write it down. Offer it up. God isn't annoyed by your repetition—He welcomes your persistence.

_____

_____

_____

_____

_____

_____

_____

5. What is one area where you need to stop performing and start trusting? Drop the act. Pick up the promise.

_____

_____

_____

_____

_____

_____

_____

Want another coloring page? I got you...

She believed God

faith like theirs

BLESSING PRAYER: For the Woman Who Believes

Gracious God,

Thank You for calling me, seeing me, and never giving up on me.

Thank You for the women who came before me: Eve, Ruth, Esther, Mary, and all the rest. They were imperfect but faithful, messy but Yours. Let their legacy become part of mine.

Lord, I don't want a faith that just *looks* good. I want one that *lives* good. One that keeps going when the feelings fade. One that clings to You when the path is dark. One that dares to believe You even when I don't understand You.

Make me bold like the bleeding woman who reached for Your robe (Mark 5:34).

Make me faithful like Hannah, praying even through tears (1 Samuel 1:15).

Make me courageous like Esther, willing to speak up and stand firm (Esther 4:14).

Make me persistent like the Canaanite woman who wouldn't let go (Matthew 15:28).

Lord, help me believe You

... not just when I'm strong, but when I'm exhausted

... not just when I see answers, but when all I see is silence

... not just in church, but in the carpool line, the workplace, and the kitchen sink moments of my real life.

I may be weary, but I'm willing. I may be broken, but I'm still Yours.

Amen.

From Devotional to Daily

What can you actually DO with all this? Here are some tangible ways to keep the fire burning after the last page:

1. Pick One Woman to Study Deeper
Choose the woman who challenged or inspired you the most. Study every verse about her. Pray through it. Journal what God is still revealing.
Pro tip: Do this once a month. Let their stories keep shaping yours.

2. Start a "She Believed God" Journal
Write down what you're praying for, what you're waiting on, and how you're watching God move—even in the quiet. (Leave space for the dates He answers you and how He does it.)

3. Gather Your Girls
Faith wasn't meant to be a solo sport. Invite a few friends to go through this study with you. Talk about what hit hard. Laugh. Cry. Eat snacks. Drink coffee. Pray like warriors.

4. Write Your Own Faith Statement
You've seen 21 different ways faith shows up. Now write yours.

> "I am a woman who believes God, even when _____. Because He is _____."

Fill it in. Put it on your mirror. Remind your heart who it belongs to.

5. Stay in the Word
You don't need a fancy plan. Just pick it up. Read a chapter a day. Or one Psalm a week. Or the Gospels slowly, with your coffee. Don't overthink it—just show up.

> *"Your word is a lamp to my feet and a light to my path."* Psalm 119:105

6. Let Grace Win
When you mess up (and you will, sorry), get back up. When you feel dry, don't quit. When shame creeps in, remind yourself: God isn't looking for perfect—He's looking for *willing*.

> *"My grace is sufficient for you, for My power is made perfect in weakness."* 2 Corinthians 12:9

And finally...

7. Walk Like You Believe Him
Not just in church. Not just when things are easy. But in every little, ordinary, sacred moment of your life. Because that's where real faith lives.

Visit www.favordeipress.com for more of my books, free, printable journaling pages, news, and to contact me for signing and speaking events

www.ingramcontent.com/pod-product-compliance
Lightning Source LLC
Chambersburg PA
CBHW070339130626

46556CB00007B/2941